LE RUOTE
La gara dell'amicizia

THE WHEELS
The Friendship Race

Inna Nusinsky

Illustrazioni di Michael Jay Roque

Illustrations by Michael Jay Roque

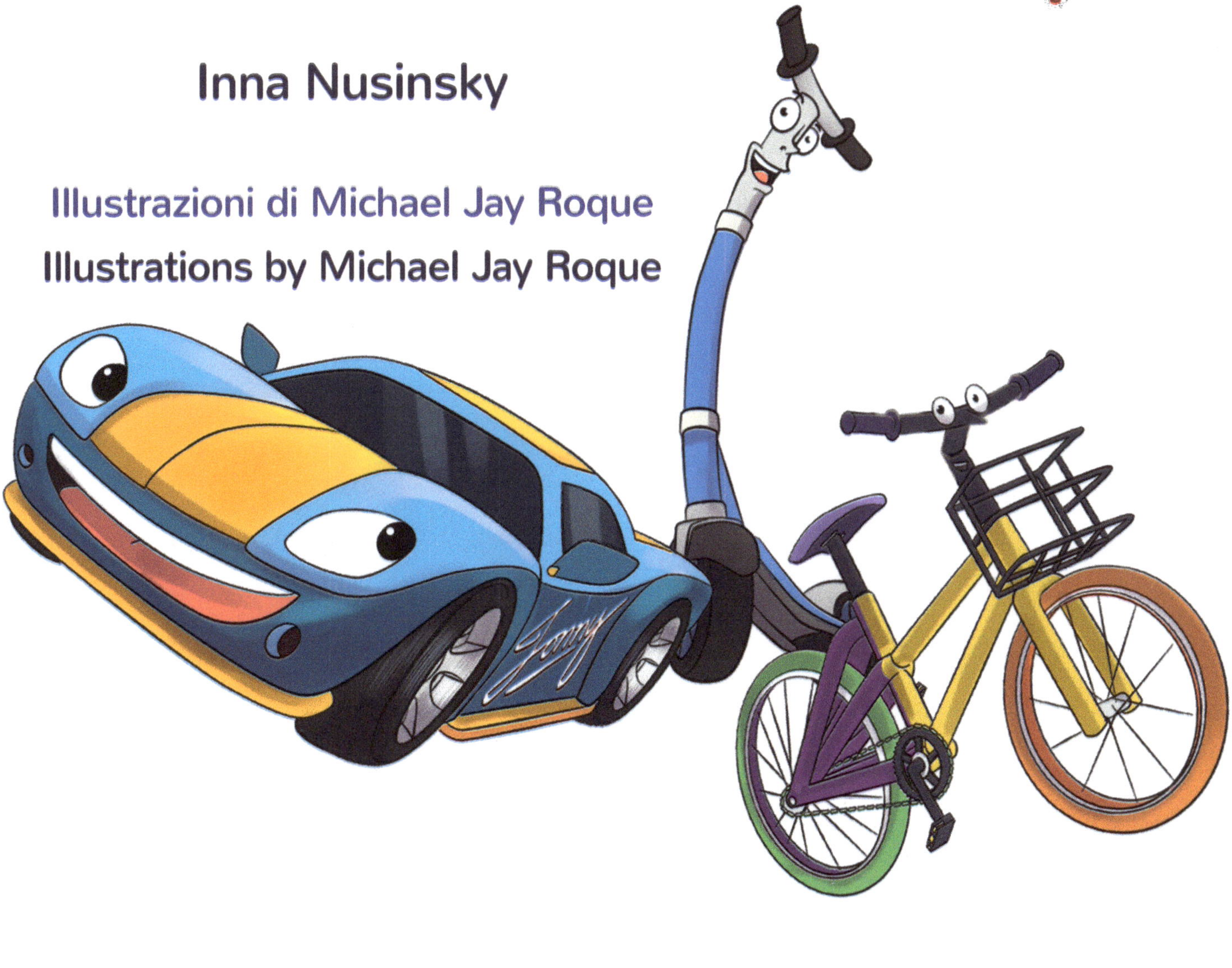

www.sachildrensbooks.com

Copyright©2015 by S.A. Publishing

innans@gmail.com

All rights reserved. No part of this book may be reproduced in any form or by any electronic or mechanical means, including information storage and retrieval systems, without written permission from the publisher or author, except in the case of a reviewer, who may quote brief passages embodied in critical articles or in a review.

Tutti i diritti sono riservati. Nessuna parte di questa pubblicazione può essere riprodotta, memorizzata in sistemi di recupero o trasmessa in qualsiasi forma o attraverso qualsiasi mezzo elettronico, meccanico, mediante fotocopiatura, registrazione o altro, senza l'autorizzazione del possessore del copyright.

First edition, 2016

Translated from English by Sara Adinolfi

Traduzione dall'inglese di Sara Adinolfi

The Wheels: The Friendship race (Italian English Bilingual Edition)
ISBN: 978-1-5259-0096-9 paperback
ISBN: 978-1-5259-0097-6 hardcover
ISBN: 978-1-5259-0095-2 eBook

Although the author and the publisher have made every effort to ensure the accuracy and completeness of information contained in this book, we assume no responsibility for errors, inaccuracies, omission, inconsistency, or consequences from such information.

Please note that the Italian and English versions of the story have been written to be as close as possible. However, in some cases they differ in order to accommodate nuances and fluidity of each language.

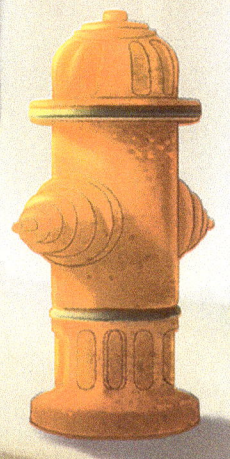

Jonny l'automobile guardò il suo riflesso nella vetrina del negozio. Com'era bello! E veloce, avrebbe potuto battere perfino le auto da corsa!
Jonny the car looked at himself in the shop window. How handsome he was! And what speed – he could beat even race cars!

"Sono l'orgoglio del quartiere," gridò.
"I'm the pride of the neighborhood," he yelled.

Mentre sognava a occhi aperti fu interrotto dal suono di due frenate.
Just then, two braking sounds broke his daydream.

Subito vide nel vetro le immagini dei suoi amici Mike la bici e Scott il monopattino.
He saw them reflected in the glass window – his friends Mike the bike and Scott the scooter.

"Ciao Jonny!" dissero gli amici. "Che succede?"
"Hey Jonny!" they said. "What's up?"

"*Ho voglia di correre un po' oggi,*" rispose Jonny, sgonfiando le gomme. "*Ma non c'è nessuno con cui posso farlo.*"

"Feeling like a little race today," said Jonny, puffing his tires. "But there's no one I can race with."

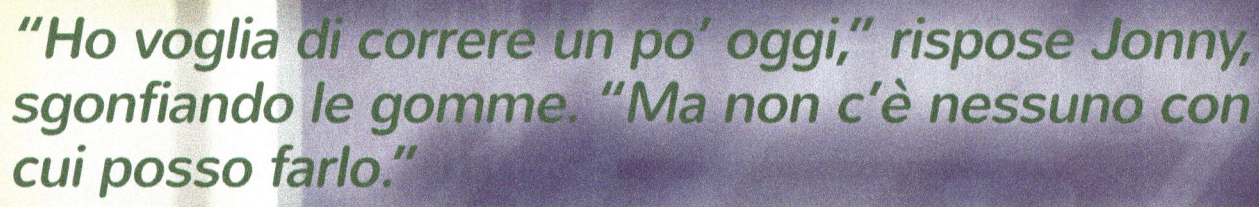

"Possiamo correre noi con te!" esclamò Mike.
"We can race with you!" exclaimed Mike.

"È a questo che servono gli amici!" aggiunse Scott.
"That's what friends are for!" added Scott.

Jonny non mostrò molto entusiasmo. "Mmm...un campione deve gareggiare con un suo simile."
Jonny didn't show much enthusiasm. "Mmm... A champion needs an equal to compete with."

Mike e Scott si scambiarono uno sguardo. I loro volti si rabbuiarono.
Mike and Scott looked at each other. A cloud passed over their faces.

"Non siamo all'altezza?" chiese Mike.
"Are we not good?" asked Mike.

"Certo che lo siete," Jonny *si guardò ancora nella vetrina. "Ma non abbastanza."*
"Oh, you're good," Jonny made a face in the glass window. "But not good enough."

"Va bene Jonny, " disse Scott. "Ti sfidiamo, facciamo una gara adesso! Facciamo tutta la Hill Road e vediamo chi arriva prima."

"Okay, Jonny," said Scott. "We challenge you to a race right now! Let's do Hill Road and see who finishes first."

Jonny fece un sorrisetto.

Jonny considered it with a smirk.

Giunti ai piedi di Hill Road la corsa ebbe inizio.
As they reached Hill Road, the race began.

C'era una salita ripida. Si sentì il rombo di Jonny che in un attimo fu in cima al pendio.
It started with a steep climb. Jonny roared and in seconds was over the incline.

Mike la bici era a metà percorso…ma il povero Scott il monopattino era senza fiato, e riuscì a salire a fatica.
Mike the bike was already half way… But poor Scott the scooter was huffing and puffing, slowly climbing up.

Jonny raggiunse l'altura e si fermò. Guardò negli specchietti retrovisori, i suoi amici erano ancora lontani.

Jonny reached the hill and stopped. He looked at the rearview mirror – his friends were far behind.

Si annoiava. Almeno la musica alla radio era di suo gusto! Chiuse gli occhi e iniziò a muoversi a ritmo.

He was bored. At least the music on the radio was good! He closed his eyes and started moving to the beat.

All'improvviso un ronzìo gli passò di fianco. C'era soltanto polvere. Mike?

Suddenly, something whirred past him and he jolted his eyes open. There was only smoke. Mike?

Prima che potesse aprire bocca, qualcos'altro lo superò. Jonny guardò nella polvere che si dissolveva, e vide Scott correre davanti a lui!

Before he could say a word something else went by. Jonny looked through the disappearing smoke—that was Scott racing ahead!

Non è possibile! Fu preso dal panico. Doveva vincere lui!

No way! Now he panicked. He should win!

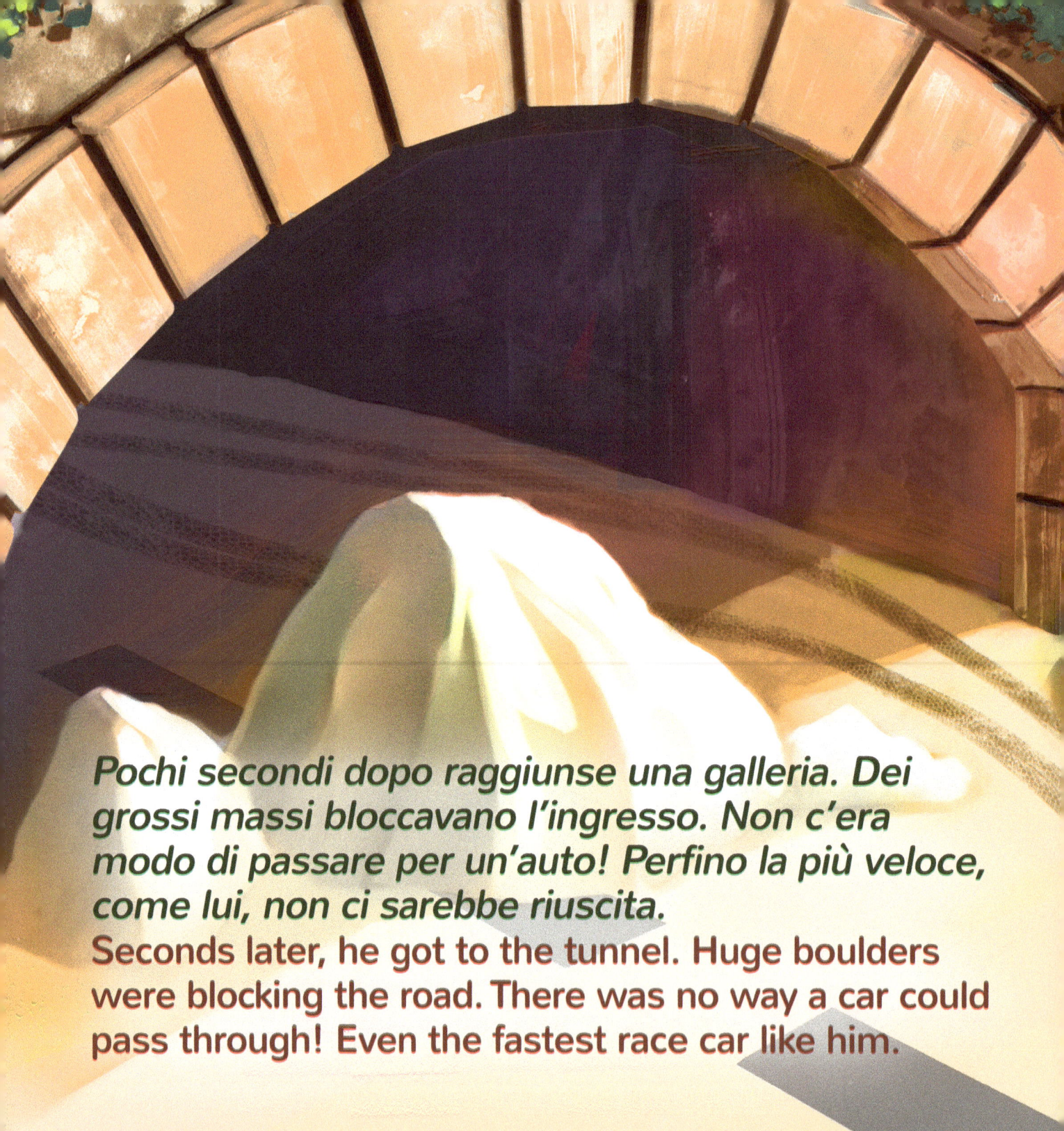

Pochi secondi dopo raggiunse una galleria. Dei grossi massi bloccavano l'ingresso. Non c'era modo di passare per un'auto! Perfino la più veloce, come lui, non ci sarebbe riuscita.

Seconds later, he got to the tunnel. Huge boulders were blocking the road. There was no way a car could pass through! Even the fastest race car like him.

Poi vide i segni delle ruote sia di Mike che di Scott. Erano riusciti a girare intorno ai massi e passare! Jonny sospirò.

But then, he saw the tire marks of both Mike and Scott. They had negotiated their way around the stone boulders! Jonny sighed.

Nel frattempo, Mike uscì dall'estremità opposta della galleria. Era in testa.

Meanwhile, Mike came out on the other side of the tunnel. He was leading.

Che razza di vittoria è, se a perdere è un tuo amico? Pensò.

What kind of a win is that when your friends lose? he thought.

Subito dopo Scott apparve al suo fianco.

In seconds, Scott was next to him.

"Perché ti sei fermato, Mike?" gli chiese. "Avresti potuto vincere la gara!"

"Why did you stop, Mike?" he asked. "You could've won the race!"

"Si ma...Jonny potrebbe essere rimasto bloccato laggiù..." disse Mike, guardando attraverso la galleria.

"Yeah but...Jonny could be stuck back there..." said Mike, looking towards the tunnel.

Ci fu un momento di silenzio.
A moment of silence passed by.

"Potremmo andare a controllare?" chiese Scott.
"Shall we go to check up him?" Scott asked.

Sul volto di Mike apparve un sorriso. "Andiamo!" disse, e si voltò.
A smile formed on Mike's face. "Let's go!" he yelled and turned back.

Davanti al passaggio bloccato Jonny era triste. Non perché stava perdendo la gara, ma perché era solo.

At the blocked tunnel, Jonny was sad. Not because he was losing the race but because he was lonely.

Poi, all'improvviso, udì un rumore di ruote. Quelli erano Scott e Mike!

Suddenly he heard a sound of wheels. Those were Scott and Mike!

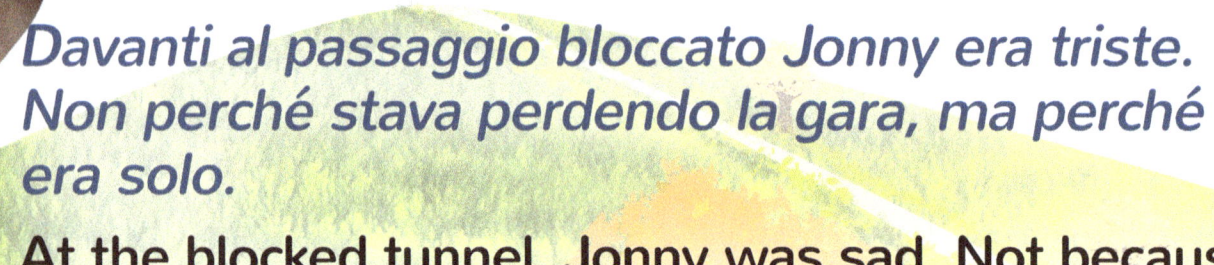

"Mike, spostiamo questi massi, così anche Jonny potrà passare!" lo incitò Scott.

"Mike, Let's move these boulders so Jonny can pass," said Scott.

I due amici iniziarono a lavorare insieme, liberando il passaggio dalle rocce.

The friends started to work together, pushing the rocks out of the way.

Non fu facile, ma, spinta dopo spinta, ci fu abbastanza spazio per far passare Jonny.

It wasn't easy, but they nudged and nudged and soon there was enough space for Jonny to squeeze through.

Ridendo, raggiunsero la fine di Hill Road.
Giggling, they reached the end of Hill Road.

"Abbiamo vinto tutti e tre!" esclamarono Mike e Scott.
"We've won the race — all of us!" exclaimed Mike and Scott.

Soltanto Jonny era un po' triste. "Mi sono comportato male con voi," ammise. "L'ho capito dopo che insieme possiamo fare molto di più. Grazie amici miei per avermelo fatto capire!"

Only Jonny was quiet. "I behaved badly with you," he admitted. "I realized it late, guys that together we can do much more. Thank you, my friends, for helping me understand that!"

Poi un applauso accolse questa splendido trio di amici...

Suddenly, there was applause, cheering for this wonderful bunch of three terrific friends...

Amici che hanno capito di essere migliori quando sono insieme.

Friends who discovered that none of them was as good as all of them.

www.ingramcontent.com/pod-product-compliance
Lightning Source LLC
Chambersburg PA
CBHW061152070526
44584CB00034B/4495